Conversations (I Never Had) With Luna and Other Stories

Anna Leah Luna-Raven

For any enquiries or permissions, the publisher can be contacted at
hello@conversationsineverhadwithluna.com

First published in Australia by: Anna Leah Luna-Raven
First Print: 2022

ASIN (e-book): B0B1YDMFPB
ISBN (paperback): 9798831292725
ISBN (hardcover): 9798831332650

Dedicated to

~

my nephews
Kim, Koko, Kiko, and Daven
~
my nieces
Danielle, Sophie, Dana, and Sabine
~
and my future daughters
Chloe and Phoebe
~
and my future sons
Zoe and Casey

Contents

Title Page

Copyright

Dedication

Introduction

~ many moons ago ~   1

cab thoughts : EMP-ty©   2

DENOUEMENT : a reprise for the New Year©   5

KUNG HEI FAT CHOI - says: the obvious choice©   8

NO.ONE SONG : FRiDOM FRiDAY... get FREE for the price of ONE©   10

CHOICES©   12

iRONY©   13

FAQs (CUES) ©   15

RETURN TO NUMBER 11~mooning over past years and the new year~©   16

GAME OF CHANCE©   17

PEEK©   19

UNTHOUGHT OF AND UNSPOKEN©   20

~ once in a blue moon ~   21

if it takes my whole life©   22

RANDOM RANTINGS: Please add me as a Friend if   23
you're not...© (The Surprise Party)

CELEBRATING RANDOMNESS©   26

...OUCH.©   27

BULLY-TIN©   30

DEAR ME©   32

DIFFERENCE©   33

DECISIONS©   35

FATE©   37

gone fishing©   38

READ BETWEEN THE LINES©   39

WEIGHT©   40

LOGIC OR HEART©   41

DRUNK©   42

HATE IS SUCH A STRONG WORD©   43

LETTER TO GOD©   46

~ over the moon ~   48

SECRET TO HAPPINESS©   49

COSMOSis©   51

LIKE THE MOON LOVES THE STARS IN THE SKY©   54

...oh i don't know... ©   58

THE ONE©   63

THROW IT OUT THERE©   64

MY NUMBERS©   65

BLESSED©   66

CONVERSATIONS (We Never Had)©   68

DISCOVERY©   71

Those Eyes©   73

WHO DO YOU LOVE?©   75

IF THE SHOE FITS©   78

MAYBE©   80

GOT TIME? ©   82

~ to the moon and back ~   83

MOONEY's SPECIAL MAGICAL SECRET GARDEN©   84

THE UNICORN SPELL©   89

GRATITUDE©   91

banana©   93

FOUR SEASONS©   94

Secret©   95

MAY MOON HAIKU©   96

NIGHT DANCE©   97

CONNECT©   98

LUNA AND STELLA©   99

~ shoot for the moon ~   105

MANTRAS©   106

WINGS©   109

KEEPING IT REAL©   110

#WAR OF WORDS©   111

I WISH©   115

BE©   117

QUESTIONS©   118

SMILE©   119

BACK TO YOU©   120

KEEP DREAMING©   122

A LETTER TO MY FUTURE CHILDREN©   124

◆◆◆   129

ABOUT THE AUTHOR   131

Connect with Me   133

Introduction

I wrote "Conversations (I Never Had) With Luna and Other Stories" while battling through depression. This poetic and narrative anthology explores the dialogues we wish to have with ourselves and others. It examines the human psyche and the dynamics of relationships, especially in the aftermath of a pandemic that has made us question our lives and survival strategies. It also offers an escape from reality, blending the past, the present, and the possible. It is divided into five chapters, each with a lunar motif : Many Moons Ago, Once in a Blue Moon, Over the Moon, Promise the Moon, and Shoot for the Moon. These chapters cover various themes, such as nostalgia, darkness, love, hope, and dreams, and aim to take the reader on an emotional and reflective journey through words.

Anna Leah Luna-Raven, May 2022

~ many moons ago ~

"I'm as old as the moon and the stars, and as young as the trees and the lakes."

Afrika Bambaataa

cab thoughts : EMP-ty©

thank you yell-OWWW taxi!

thank you play on words.
thank you afterthought.
here i am on my way home.
on my way back.
and here i am.
on my way to thinking
about you.
catching myself before
i completely do.
thank you.
for the temporary calm.
for the (temporary) respite.
for this temporary cave.
from the maddening world
from this crazy world.
temporary though,
i say,
for i know for a fact
that there will
come a time when
they will find out
about you.
am not supposed to put this
into writing
for fear that they might use this
to find you
but still decided to do so
lest i myself
forget.
about you.

this is a reprise of
the denouement.
over and again.
never ends,
does it?
thank you my
big.
thank you
song.
thank you premonition.
thank you no. 25.
thank you paris.
thank you for curbing your enthusiasm.
and your pain.
and everything else.
would you like to hear
about mine?
thank you for the
unexplained silence.
thank you bruno.
have you gotten
yours yet?
thank you long wait.
the other shoe fell.
the loose tooth fell off.
thank you,
my heart
did drop too.
thud, it said.
thank you broken heart ---
OWWW.
and still having to owe.
thank you unfair trade.
you said so yourself.
after all,
you can't always get
a free ride.
thank you what-not.
trying to make a big decision.
with the meter running,

thank you.
thank you limit.

thank you for the ride.
this is me.
getting off now.
keep the change.

DENOUEMENT : *a reprise*

for the New Year©

Up. Down.
Up and about.
Still trying to find
A fitting end to the start
How then?
Let's begin again…

This game has long been over

And now,
I'm looking
to forever.

I still don't know you.

And you still don't know me.

Though we've known

each other all along.

I'm still trying to recover
From getting through
And from making sense,
Making time,
Making rhyme.

Maybe you're still trying to

Make this about
you,

Whenever it suits
you…
Or about me,

Whenever you feel uneasy…

You want it to turn out the way

you want

While I try

To sit it out and wait...

For you to
get over it,
Over yourself
...and do the dodge
So as not to offend
Whether you,
Or me
Or the others
watching
And wondering
as well
How the curve
will go
How the slope
would turn
Are you there?
And then
I start to laugh
And cry
And be myself
Again.
From hereon
now,
The end
begins.

Happy New Year stranger.

Is it?
sniff
Salvation must have found you.
because i didn't see you there.

Was it everything you
expected it to be?

Did you find what you were
looking for?

KUNG HEI FAT CHOI -

says: the obvious choice©

we all put special value on
different things...

a note.
that's with a trinket.
that's in a box.
...regardless of the price, the cost.

and we all put special value on
different people...

family.
wives, husbands sons, daughters,
grandchildren
pets
friends.
old and new
around the neighborhood,
in school,
at work
significant others.
boyfriends, girlfriends
lovers
fiances, fiancees
... regardless of names, age, sexual orientation,
color, race, religion

and we all put special value on ideas, on feelings
--- tangible or not.

LOVE
HAPPINESS
RESPECT

And all this?
invaluable.
priceless.

what we consider
special, meaningful
is up to each of us...

a child's laugh
an old person's smile
a parent's advice
a friend's hug
a hand to hold.

the world and its mysteries,
--- not understanding
all of them
but being part of it.
being alive.

this note,
notes.
FREEDOM.
now put a price on that.

Kung Hei Fat Choi. (Happy New Year)

and Happy Independence day.

𝒩𝒪.𝒪𝒩ℰ 𝒮𝒪𝒩𝒢 : FRiDOM FRiDAY... get FREE for the price of ONE©

black.
darkness.
void. emptiness.
that was me.

white.
cleansing.
purity. blank.
that was you.

negra. blanco.

the keys have lost their tune
no more melody
no more harmony

we used to be so good together
good for each other
make good music together.

we used to fill each other's
emptiness.

and each other's song lines
and verses.

we were pieces of
teclado. you. me.
and the spaces in between.

now there are colors that
go better with you.
and some,
better with me.
like some notes
have no need for a sharp
or a flat.
now the keys have gone
out of tune.

there used to be little space in
between.
now the spaces have grown they seem b i g g e r
--- between each octave.
so i guess you're free to go now.

so am i...
like i am.

that was 10 years at the least. after all.

ok, so this was for
you. so what?

CHOICES©

Do you choose love or love chooses you?
What if you choose to love and then end up hurt again?

And what if you let love
choose you,
Would you wait 'til forever?

Take me for a ride
because it is making me smile, at least.
But eventually I'll have to get off somewhere.

And you will drive again.
Drive away, alone.

And I, I will walk,
taking small steps instead of a hundred miles per hour.

And although alone I walk,
I have sights around me to see.

And you shall pass them by, because
you don't stop or slow down for any sign.

iRONYc

goin' b A n a N a S !

i am a paradox of sorts, my own antithesis...

cowboy and sassy, metal and mush, the tamer and the tamed, the one who was left behind and the one who got away, wallflower and butterfly, sea creature and heavenly body, a child squeezed into an adult... i smile a lot my jaws hurt... can be a bit of a (uhmmm, big) klutz... somehow, almost always fashionably late... i am too darn cynical due to the many times i've been burned and the scars left thereafter but can be too hopefully idealistic for my own good at times... kind of nocturnal but loves waiting for the sun to come up...

i love fiery sunsets and walks on the beach, chilled beer after a hard day's work, long baths, watching the rain through misty windows, snuggling in bed during a storm, bear hugs, pig outs and laugh trips, long drives, impromptu meetings, a good book, coffee just about any time of the day, surprises, krispy kreme doughnuts, tiger and damper buns, a strong cosmopolitan or bellini, shopping!, staring up at my star-streaked sky, good vibes, playing matchmaker to my friends but still haven't found the one who can put up with all of my idiosyncrasies (uhmmm, he hasn't found me i guess)...

i believe in the good in all people and that nobody is born evil...a self-confessed drama queen and try-hard comedian, an accident waiting to happen, a sucker for love and life and anything in between, a gypsy that's lived through so much i wouldn't know where to begin, often wonders about what might have been and what lies ahead i constantly have to remind myself to live in the NOW...

13

favorite questions: who are you? and what is the meaning of
life?

...my friends reckon i'm crazy, i say bloody oath, mate.

$\mathcal{FAQ}_s$ (CUES) ©

why do we close our eyes
      when we cry?
      or
      touch our chest
      when it hurts?
      or
      put our head in our hands
      when confused?
why do we shake our legs
      when we're waiting?

For answers to come.
For clarity.
    To make sure
    our heart's still there
    To shut out the pain.

RETURN TO NUMBER

11 ~ mooning over past years and the new year ~ ©

why would i want to do that?
why would anyone want to do that?
what would YOU say?
what would YOU do?
how would YOU feel?

looking back in hindsight,
did it feel right?
would you go back
to number 11?

would you go back to number 11?
when you started school and
first fell in love
where all events,
big and small,
first came to life
and turned into wonderful memories

why would i NOT want to do that?
why would anyone NOT want to do that?
what would I say?
what would I do?
how would I feel?

GAME OF CHANCE©

Isn't it funny
how randomness
can be so Un-random?
Predictable, even?

If things happen to certain people,
And we get told that
everything happens for a reason,
Then isn't that contradicting?

If we were to take Karma into
consideration,
And as we all know,
Karma is just the result of
what you put out into the world,
Then isn't it contradicting to say
That things just happen randomly to people?

That we are only treated
poorly or nicely
Because we have been
the same way to others?

Now, take two strangers

finding each other

Somehow coming into

each other's lives

Getting to know each other

Talking to each other

Somehow being available,

in some weird way,

For each other

at the same time

Understanding each other

Would you call that randomness too?

Or, does it all feel so
Contrived?
Planned?
Organized?

Would you feel like some strange force
has put you right on the spot?
Like putting certain people
In our lives
And letting certain events Happen…

Is it a game of chance?
Is it Destiny?
How would you call it?

 PEEK©

You wanted me to show
you my world.

Well, here it is...
A little peek
into my world so far.

Do you like what you
see?

UNTHOUGHT OF *and* UNSPOKEN©

I would love to tell someone
What I really think or feel
If only I could.

Well, why the hell not,
 you'd say.
 I have no idea.

I guess some things are
better off unspoken,
or
unthought of.

Forget it, and
move on.

The sooner, the
better.

Did I just say that out loud?

~ *once in a blue moon* ~

"*Every one is a moon, and has a dark
side which he never shows to anybody*"

Mark Twain

if it takes my whole life©

drab and dragging.
satire-agedy /slash/ tra-tire
(more satiric than tragic).

like squeezing lime on a wound after downing
painkillers with vodka --- senseless and unnecessary.
like a pejorative
comment.
not at all impressive.
neither enticing.
nor worthy of wow...

but you catch yourself
sitting there wanting to
know more,and realize you
want to hear more, nd end
up watching more.
...an effort definitely worth the title.

RANDOM RANTINGS:
Please add me as a Friend if you're not...© (The Surprise Party)

Please add me as a Friend if you're not...

.. the backstabbing b*tch that set-up a surprise birthday party for my then boyfriend whom you've had the hots for ever since, and then never told me about it until i found out from my sister because you had the nerve to invite her too and yet not think "omg, what if she told her and found out?" because you were too busy thinking up ways to snatch him right from under my nose, so i ended up looking like a great, big fool after i spent the whole day racking my brains out and going around to look for that perfect present for him

... who was actually successful in making us break up, though he doesn't know that was one of the many reasons, among other things

... who turned him and our friends against me by bad-mouthing me not in the most discreet of ways but by being oh-so-unbelievably-fake-plastic-boobs-charming while you're at it, and who always manages to turn things around by using psych-sh*t experiments on me so i'd feel sad and envious and then angry at myself and not you, that some bigwig's pending ethics case would be put to shame

... and who thinks she knows me but obviously not well enough to remember that i rarely ever talk, if at all. and that this venting out is called t h e r a p y. or have you forgotten that too?

... who, before you think you're that important to have a note written about, i hope does not suffer from short attention span anymore though so you can read the disclaimer at the end of this

... and who for the love of God, is still trying to convince yourself you have a happy marriage but just had to name one of your kids (weren't you the one who asked to leave the kids ---or anyone else not involved for that matter--- out of complicated "grown-up, mature" stuff?) after my above-mentioned then boyfriend several years after (unless...omg, I'm not going there), and secretly raving about the fact that neither one of us has him now

... and who i think is still punishing me for not making you use the name i had picked out first back when we were kids playing make-believe, and for not swapping that special stationary my grandma gave me with you

... who thinks it's still ok to be friends after I've missed crucial moments which I cannot get back and lost several years of my life (which is about the same amount of time it took yourself to get married and pregnant, bear that full-term, and celebrate many birthdays, holidays and other special occasions with family and friends) in isolation like you have no idea, no thanks to you

... and who still cannot come to terms with the fact that you are older than I am and therefore need to know better too (but you're reading this anyways so that pretty much says everything)

... who, while you're probably right in thinking that i have no clue of the joys and pains of being a mother, must know too that that experience can only be worthwhile if you teach by example and you follow-through

... and who thinks you know all about friendship AND love but doesn't realize that had you been totally honest about it in the past, you would have gotten the love you longed for AND still have a friend in me, but sadly never really understood it was NOT either friendship OR love

... who wants forgiveness but is too proud or afraid to ask for it

... who is trying to get into my life once again and probably cooking up another evil plot to get to me and ruin my otherwise peaceful life (which is more than what I can say for you)

... and who just can't seem to be happy for others, and i pray that you learn that anger is so pointless and senseless and drains so much of our energy which can be channeled into more fruitful endeavors, like say, this note --- so get over it

... and who is giving me a really hard time trying to keep to my mantras: "always be good even if others are not" and "the best way to say something is to not say anything at all"

phew.

yeah, and you're realizing this just now.

... otherwise, get a life. i mean get on with your life. go on now... move along...

CELEBRATING
RANDOMNESS©

* This story is based on / inspired by actual events.

* The events depicted in this note are fictitious. In certain cases incidents, characters and timelines have been changed for dramatic purposes.

* Any similarity or resemblance to real person/s, living or dead, is unintentional and merely coincidental. Certain characters may be composites, or entirely fictitious.
..Or I wish they were.

* This article does not reflect the thoughts or opinions of either myself, my real friends, or my dog.*(Hopefully) No real b*tches were harmed before, during and after the writing of this note. They're either too dense or too insensitive for that.

* Reader assumes full responsibility. Brains not included.

* For recreational use only. This note, dimwit... not me.

...OUCH.©

Dear W,

You have no right to hurt me this way. There are only a few people who can hurt me, and that would not include you. There would only be one person who can make me cry, and it would not be you.

I have a longtime crush who I have always been fond of for several years now. Eight years to be exact. Every time I go to my usual cafe, I order for two --- one for me and the other for later, which I would leave for him. It doesn't matter whether it's the shop in the northern suburbs, or the one in the South, I send him text messages to pick up the coffee along with the gift I leave for him every single time. Of course, since he has no idea who I am, I was expecting him not to give notice to whatever it is I was doing. But still, I was half-expecting him to... even for a bit. I even made a scrapbook for him wherein I wrote a month's worth of cards, a handful of quotes and little notes with my memories of when we saw or bumped into each other, and some movie and song inspirations. Of course, in it were also some of the receipts of the coffee that I got for him --- coffees that we hadn't had together. That was my New Year's gift for him. But like those other times, he did not pick it up. Ouch. Stupid, right? So anyways, it turned out he had a girlfriend, and she even called me up to ask me to stop texting him regarding the coffees. I wanted to tell her too bad she didn't think about doing that for him, but then again, I did not. Maybe he felt it was too much. So I still have the scrapbook, the collectible planner I got for all those coffees, and a few extra bitter memories to write down on them ---all to remind me of the rejection I got from him.

And then there's this married guy I'm seeing right now. He has *secret* kids from his *secret* other relationships and has other "flaws" that I would not even dare elaborate on. And I knew it from the onset of the "pseudo-relationship." He's five years older, also a Gemini like I am, and stubborn at that. By the way, to top it all off, his present wife is my friend's *secret*...so that's that. Otherwise, everything's perfect. We had a happy out of town weekend together, and I couldn't ask for anything more. But then I did. So now, I'm screwed. Of course, he could not possibly give me as much time and attention as he would like to (given the benefit of the doubt that he would really want to) because of his family. I feel really guilty because of the simple fact that I never imagined I would risk almost twenty years of friendship over him, or choose him over that --- though it seems that I have done just that. I don't even know why I fell for him...he snores, a bit less of a gentleman, childish and he hurts me emotionally though he never realizes it. One time I tried to hold his hand and he let go, afraid someone might see. Ouch. I keep running through my mind the scene when I would finally just tell him: "go home to your wife and kid/s," but I can't find myself to do it. I feel like he's still in this just to be polite. Or afraid that I might tell on him. So, I come across as that shallow... Ouch.

I have another married man friend whom I chat with all the time, but oddly is never there whenever I need a friend the most. Ouch. I have an ex-boyfriend who I have invited to be a friend over Facebook, but has not approved or confirmed it yet. Ouch. I have job applications I failed to pass and dreams that haven't been realized. Ouch. I get unanswered calls, I send text messages and emails that never get responded to. Ouch. I get tired of being second-best. Ouch.

So you see, you sitting on your black swivel chair in your fancy posh office texting me to stop texting you is nothing compared to what I've been through, and still am going through every single day. I eat rejection for breakfast, and sadly even crave for it sometimes I have it for lunch, and by the time dinner comes, I had already been addicted to it. I would gladly swap crème brulee or tiramisu for it as dessert. Because there is no other thing on the menu.

So don't --- never think that you hurt me. Why would you think that? You surely don't know I left at that time because of you... And never mind the time you asked me if I was happy... Would you be able to do anything if I'm not? Nothing.

Ouch...

BULLY-TIN©

In your smile, all pain and bitterness is hidden.
Every word you hear seems like a bullet
piercing through your body.
Every punch adds one more day of terror.
Every laugh lets one more tear escape.
Every insult is another wound and scar.

You can't escape it.
You're trapped in their judgment because
this determines who you are.
You're who they say you are.
Just like a puppet controlled by a puppeteer.

You keep hiding,
but they still find ways to find
every flaw that would slowly start to destroy you.
How much more can you take before you break?

As the day passes another part of you fades.
Little by little you feel yourself disappearing.
Alone in this dark and quiet night filled with sadness,
you question yourself.

Leaving you restless,
Sleepless nights thinking of what's wrong with you.
She's so ugly! Does she think she's pretty?
What an attention seeker.

You're drowning in the sea of your tears
and no one's there to save you.

When will this end?
I'm tired.
Soon enough you won't find anything
To criticize, oppress, hurt and gossip about
I will find a way to disappear

Please don't miss me when
I'm gone.
Don't even look for me.
Because that time
you do,
I will have been swallowed
By my own tears,
by my own cries of pain
Underneath the ground.

What are those tears for?
Newsflash: You hear them say, she made her
take her own life.
She isn't worthy to be here.
Do you feel that?
Pain, anguish and embarassment.
Have you become me?
My mother always said,
What goes around comes around.

Where are you now?
You said, don't miss me when I'm gone.
Don't even look for me. They don't.
You are just a number, just another one of us now.

DEAR ME©

You are the elephant in
the room

No one can speak of you
Or talk to you
You don't exist
Your mere presence is doom

Dear Stranger
Do you know?
Would you tell me what's happening
I have no idea
Should I leave it, drop it
And keep pretending.

Dear Stranger's Friend
(elephant sound)
You seem to know.
Know me.

DIFFERENCE©

How do we differentiate what's
right from wrong
Because what's right may not be good
and what's wrong may not be bad

And then
what might be good ---
might not be good for everyone.

I am completely lost.

I want to do something.

But I'm afraid
I will make the wrong choice
and
I am afraid
I will not do good

Torn.

That is why I end up doing nothing.

That is why I am always upset
That is why I always feel bad
That is why I keep eating my
own words
That is why I end up hurting people

That is why I always ask

    but never get any answers.

How is it that it's everybody else's business except my own?

DECISIONS©

It is so easy to judge a person

    because of the choices he or she makes.

      It is so easy because we are not in that person's shoes

What if we were, what do we do?

    Where do we base our decisions

    if there are no facts presented to
us?

    What do we do?
How do we make a supposedly
"intelligent" decision?
an informed decision?

And if we make a decision,

    and presented with the facts later on,

    How do we make the necessary change?

    How do we repair the damage?

I guess no matter what we choose
we're bound to hurt someone in the end.

People don't want honesty or your truth.
They want you to admit you're someone you're not,
they want to hear what they want to.

They want their truth,
so you end up being a liar

whatever you say or do anyways.

HATE©

happy are the
lucky ones
lonely are the
doomed. they
bleed
they hurt

they tear and
fall apart they
scream,
they die...

happy are my
friends, lonely
am

i.

gone fishing©

Love is non-existent.

Love has no part in
the game.

Too bad you got the
wrong fish.

READ BETWEEN
THE LINES©

Have you read it?

Why didn't I get the memo?

WEIGHT

I feel so fat,

From
eating

My own
words.

Yes,
heavy.

Take this
weight off
my shoulders.

LOGIC *OR HEART*©

Would you rather

lose logic?

Or

lose heart?

DRUNK

We make our own coffee
at times,

Sometimes, we pay for
our own coffee

But we drink our own
coffee,

All the time.

My heart is beating fast.

$\mathcal{HATE}$ IS SUCH A STRONG WORD©

I'm beginning to hate airplanes
I'm beginning to hate parking lots
 I'm beginning to hate puking
I'm beginning to hate the rain
I'm beginning to hate cars, big cars, small cars, fast cars
I'm beginning to hate convoys
I'm beginning to hate airports
I'm beginning to hate TV and radio
I'm beginning to hate my computer
I'm beginning to hate food, or what's in it
I'm beginning to hate the air,
the smell around me like smoke
I'm beginning to hate going out
I'm beginning to hate having to go out
I'm beginning to hate birthdays
I'm beginning to hate the number 10
I'm beginning to hate talking
I'm beginning to hate other names
 I'm beginning to hate myself
I'm beginning to hate hating
I'm beginning to hate men - or boys
I'm beginning to hate carpenters
I'm beginning to hate my voice
I'm beginning to hate running around in circles
I'm beginning to hate videos
I'm beginning to hate Coca-Cola, or any soft drink for that matter

I'm beginning to hate being cynical
I'm beginning to hate being overly idealistic or
being hopelessly romantic
I'm beginning to hate not knowing anything
I'm beginning to hate not being told anything
I'm beginning to hate the letter C and K
I'm beginning to hate time
I'm beginning to hate paranoia
I'm beginning to hate my hair
I'm beginning to hate my moods
I'm beginning to hate hospitals
I'm beginning to hate being pushed around
I'm beginning to hate my whining
I'm beginning to you being bitchy
I'm beginning to hate people who think they know me
I'm beginning to hate noise
I'm beginning to hate silence - makes me uncomfortable
I'm beginning to hate shopping
I'm beginning to hate the blue book
I'm beginning to hate you
... and you and you
I'm beginning to hate the past
I'm beginning to hate having to live in the present
I'm beginning to hate the future
I'm beginning to hate travelling of any sort
I'm beginning to hate departures, including mine
I'm beginning to hate death
I'm beginning to hate old age
I'm beginning to hate my migraines
I'm beginning to hate the sky
I'm beginning to hate manipulation
I'm beginning to hate all things I love
I'm beginning to hate phone calls, missed calls, messages

I'm beginning to hate goodbyes
I'm beginning to hate hellos -
because they eventually end up in goodbyes too
I'm beginning to hate writing
I'm beginning to hate superheroes
I'm beginning to hate any kind of feeling
I'm beginning to hate acting fine when I'm not
I'm beginning to hate this list
because it's longer than the list of things I love.

I'm beginning to hate falling in love again.

LETTER *To God*©

Dear God,

I don't think I would want to be you. I'm sorry, please don't take that the wrong way. I wonder how my parents would feel if they knew what I go through every day. I'm sure it would break their hearts knowing that their child is having such a difficult time coping. It's not even about this damn disease or illness. It was even way before that.

I know how difficult it must have been for you, knowing your Son suffered a lot, even from people He cared so much about. I am no saint, not even close to that. I have feelings too. I know how much it must have hurt to see your Son be betrayed, be let down, be rejected, be turned back on, be denied, be spit on, be laughed at, be tortured, be mocked, be oppressed, be criticized, be tripped or stepped on, be humiliated, and be nailed to the Cross.

More than Jesus's own feelings, I wondered how You, His Father, and Mary, His Mother, must have felt. Did you close your eyes and just wish those things weren't happening, wish them away?

I wondered, too, since You are God, who did You run to? Who did You pray to and ask for help? Was it difficult knowing You're alone? And that You couldn't do much to help?

I wondered, too if these people who hurt Your Son ever thought about their own brother/s or sister/s? Or their parents? Or their friends?

I wondered if they thought about the many nights that You stayed up til late, hoping Your Son was alright wherever He was. I wondered if they thought about the many thoughts You had about what Your Son was doing --- whether He has already eaten, or is already safely on the way home, what He and His friends (the few He had, if He had any real ones at all) were talking about.

I wondered if they knew that Your Son had the same thoughts You had about them too, that He was hoping they were all fine.

But then again, why should that be their problem?

I'm sorry, God, I don't think I would want to be you.

~ *over the moon* ~

"yours is the light by which my spirit's born:
yours is the darkness of my soul's return
- you are my sun, my moon,
and all my stars"

e.e.cummings

SECRET TO
HAPPINESS©

Want to know a secret? Mine is you.

My most favourite day was when I met you, as if on fate's cue.

Happy, happy! I am feeling the best ever!
I found me a beautiful chappy. What could be better?

I saw the sun was especially bright and the sky was unbelievably blue.
I heard the bees buzzing and the birds singing
their sweet song.
The trees and the flowers smelt lovely too.
The air felt cool and the breeze so strong.
The tiny raindrops tasted like honeydew.
And that's when you came along.

That was
Happiness.

Then came
Joy.

Joy is seeing the azure sky speaking to me through the white feathery cotton clouds above this lovely country.
Looking at the sun, never did it shine as dazzling and brilliant so.
Hello it said, the yellow makes me not a tad bit mellow.
My mind at ease.
Yet funny, I wonder, has anyone heard a bee sneeze?
Why haven't I listened to the skylark's delightful melody before?
Now I'm craving the tune and oh, for so much more.

Joy, over and yonder, is when I get a whiff of the citrusy
fragrance of pine trees.

Of charming roses and lavender, I could make enchantingly-
scented posies.
I can almost touch the crisp air with my bare hands.
The breeze enveloped me, so intense, it felt like quicksand.

Pitter patter, little dewdrops that hop
A mix of bitter, sweet, salty, sour, savoury, its flavour just pops.
Suddenly, I found a deeper meaning around me, about
everyone and everything.
With a rollercoaster of emotions, I wonder, Am I
dreaming?

Breathing in the aroma of home-baked bread,
Examining and tapping the cracks on its head,
Stroking and caressing the lines, contours and marks,
Listening to the crack and crunch when I break it apart,
Savouring the salt, yeast and butter,
it has so much to offer and then, thinking
--- oh, what a joy!

Joy, joy! I am going to burst!
I found not a boy. But, it could have been worse.
When I found me is my most favourite time.
Want to know a secret? I am mine.

COSMOSis©

Who are you, stranger?
Are you the one watching over me when the day ends?
When the sun hides and you magically appear just around the
bend?
Your imperfections make you perfect.
Full, crescent, new, waxing and waning.
Wistfully, I try to fathom your whole being.

What beauty is she?
Glittery light shining from her face,
the Moon turns in a steady pace.
Looking down at the end of the hustle of our daily race.
Silver dust gathered over her face -
beguiling, charming, mesmerizing.
Constant, calm, silent, full of wonder to me.
She is changed but unchanging.

When do you come out?
When she hears the cheerful sound of children playing
hide-and-seek laughing in the Twilight
A gentle melody of owls and wolves and crickets and frogs at
night.
When she sees the bonfire, and the aimless wandering of
lovers out of plain sight.
In my dreams, the good ones and bad, and when I hug the one
who tucks me in and reads me bedtime stories tonight.

Where do you live?
Where the moonbeam falls between mountains and valleys,
and on the horses' stables,
In the sand and waves crashing in the sea,
influencing ebbs and flows and tides alike
Where glass is carefully shaped when lighting strikes
And the soul and spirit in your eyes sparkle.

How are you, Moon?
Has anyone ever asked you that?
Not only do you look and listen to everyone's
happiness and joy, misery and woes about life
But you pause, think, and reflect,
and show no interest to engage in idle chat.
Sometimes you remind me of a noble, polite and lovely wife.

Why do you do what you do?
Do you know, she said, who knows you and loves you anyways?
Look out your window and look up.
I can, I will keep your secret, says the Moon,
her heart in full display.
I know all of them.
Now sleep, my child, rest and stop.

But do you not get tired of all the stories that you keep?
Are you not bound to burst from all the worry of all the
troubles you bear?
Yes, I do, says the Moon. I cry too and let out tears,
heart on my sleeve I wear.
Don't you see them all around you, up in the Sky with me,
and count them like sheep? Do you not call them Stars?

And that's when we became reflections of you...
We became you. Your light, your darkness,
your ambiguity, your constancy.
Your love, your passion, your life, your inspiration.
Little glimmers of hope in you, of you.
Distant, yet near. Alone, but never really lonely.

Do you not see?
The sky is our perpetual backdrop, in splendid deep shades and
hues of pink, purple and blue.
The clouds form your thoughts, bubbles of ideas which are
your mind's fruits.
Madness, and explosions, and little triumphs, and evolution,
and truth.
All of it. Plus you.

Do you not hear? Do you not know?
Do you not understand signs when stars align?
We're joined in this time-bound thread we call night.
Yet night turns into day, when the sun wakes you from your
dream.

Life, made of night and day, sun and moon, stars and clouds,
and everything in the universe, tell I might.
Life, this link, this connection, is timeless..
it all makes sense, or so it seems.
So, for now, Goodnight.

LIKE THE *moon* LOVES THE *Stars* IN THE *Sky*©

"Mummy, how much do you love me?" asks Stella.

"I love you to the moon and back, baby,"

her mummy, Luna, replies.

See this black, round teeny-weeny mole?

Mummy had it when she was very young.

She was just like you, a special gift, a little jewel,

Tiny and gentle and precious.

See this lumpy, red line?

Mummy got it when I gave birth to you,

My belly was big when you were inside,

And after you were born, it became smaller as you grew.

See this patchy, rough, burnt spot?

Mummy had it when I was heating the kettle,

So I could get you your milk bottle.

The water spit and it hurt like hell.

See this jagged, crusty scar?

Mummy got it when our puppy, Peppa scratched me.

She was upset and lonely,
Because she was jealous of you, our new baby.

See this crooked, zigzagy wrinkle?
Mummy got it on your first day of school
Because I was scared and anxious and lost my cool,
But I had to let go, so Dad gave me a pull.

See this dry, coarse grey hair?
Mummy gets them for every homework
That you and I do together and is one of mum's perks
When mum thinks it shows, it's like a family quirk

See these ugly scabs on my legs and blisters on my feet?
Aches and pain and stinging they bring
But I enjoy our walks on the beach and the park and the street
that I wouldn't trade them for anything.

So you see, my child, I love you.
Like the moon loves the stars in the sky.

The moon has imprints of every moment,
every milestone,
every special occasion
that they share together.
Every crater or hole or spot on her face has a story to tell
As a reminder, of how she loved the stars with a passion.

Mummy isn't perfect, baby.
She has marks, and spots and lines on her face and body.
But they are a reminder of you too and

how precious you are to me.
Because I love you and care for you, I also share this story.

These marks and spots and lines create a constellation.
Of you, me, us and the family together, our every emotion
Like a light, they will guide you through, whatever your location
and will be cause for every celebration.

It's now getting late, time for bed
Rest your tiny sleepy head
Tomorrow we'll speak again
while I am on the train

Now, blow me a kiss And make a little wish

That someday soon I won't have to miss

Your other firsts, like when you catch your first
fish or cook your first dish

Though we're apart
For as long as you're in my heart
And I'm in yours, God will open doors

Goodnight, my dear

Hush, wipe those tears and do not fear

Mummy will be home soon
We'll be together again soon, and I'll always be near.

"Mummy, how much do you love me?" "I love you to the moon
and back, baby"

"Baby, how much do you love me?"

"I love you to the moon, and Come back, Mummy."

...oh i don't know... ©

what does he know about not meeting expectations
--- or not having any?
what does he know about setting expectations ---
and expecting one too many?
what does he know about hurt?
About pain? About anguish?
what does he know about truth ---
when all he's ever been told was a lie?
what does he know about having to lie
to get to the truth?
what does he know about being a friend,
when he couldn't even understand me
as an enemy, a stranger, an employee?
what does he know about ranting and raving?
what does he know about being both
the boon and bane of existence?
what does he know about not getting the answers you
expected?
what does he know about failure?
About frustration? About rejection?
what does he know about falling in love ---
with all the wrong people?
under the most unusual of circumstances?
what does he know about wanting to fall in love,
but just can't?
what does he know about NOT
wanting to fall in love,
but just can't help it?
what does he know about distraction?
what does he know about trust?

what does he know about fear?
what does he know about making yourself a bait,

waiting for the shark to come smell your blood
and swim after you

--- and fearing it is going to eat you alive?
what does he know about trying to fill
a position, an emptiness, a void?
what does he know about trying to fill up time?
or making up for the loss of it?

what does he know about missing someone

--- when there was hardly ever anyone?
what does he know about losing everything
you ever had or has ever meant something to you?
what does he know about getting or not getting
what you deserve?
what does he know about sudden appearances,
and flashes of light?
And having your whole life appear before your eyes?
what does he know about putting up with other people's shit?
and swallowing your pride?

and counting the days til it will be all over?

what does he know about making decisions,

when you're left with not much of a choice?
what does he know about waking up the next day,
wishing it'll be better?
what does he know about the good times
and the bad times,
and the otherwise mundane times?
what does he know about not making sense
--- yet be perfectly understood?
what does he know about being misunderstood
--- when you haven't really spoken much?
what does he know about talking to myself?
and have to hear it from other people?
what does he know about
the seven-year itch, middle-age crisis or second childhood

and the other inconveniences or phenomena

that we have and use as, for lack of a better term, excuses?
what does he know about blind faith?

what does he know about never quite making it?

what does he know about plans
not being carried out or seen to fruition?

what does he know about dreams not being realized?

what does he know about not knowing when
to give up or give in?

or when never to let go?
what does he know about loneliness,
in a room full of people?
--- and have someone say they've been there,
but know that they have no idea what that is like?

what does he know about wanting to say all
the right things

--- and end up with the most stupid lines?
what does he know about love and
life, and everything in between?
and know you're going to get something
you've already heard before?
what does he know about love
and all the crazy things you do for it?
what does he know about mystery?

and the feeling you get

that just when you think you've got it all figured out,

something comes along that completely surprises you ---
and you don't quite know what to do?

what does he know about being out of your comfort zone?

what does he know about magic and ever-after,
and what comes afterwards?

what does he know about being lost?

what does he know about wanting to come home?

and not knowing where that is?
what does he know about not knowing
who to ask for directions?
what does he know about getting wrapped up in a fantasy
world
--- and actually just wanting to stay there?
for the very reason that
you have nowhere else to go?

what does he know about having someone totally upset you,

without really knowing why?

or unable to say why?

what does he know about pent-up feelings
and mixed emotions,

and ending up drunk,
and saying the most inappropriate things,
and kicking yourself in the butt the day after?
what does he know about me
--- going on and on and on...
about what I think he does not know
and is similarly looking for answers to?

or about what I think he already knows but
would not tell me?

what does he know about keeping secrets?
what does he know about firsts and lasts,
and keeping memories ---
and having people steal them from you?
and how you hear people say ---
"wow, that's gotta hurt..."?

what does he know about
betrayal?

what does he know about
conscience?
and how we're always searching for ways to live without it
so we can keep our sanity?
and how we're always searching for it
whenever we need to keep someone else sane?
what does he know about keeping something for years,

and the moment you decide

to try to open up your heart a little bit,

having it broken again?
what does he know about trying to
find yourself
--- and in the process,
finding someone else
who meant a lot to someone?

what does he know about wasted opportunities?

what does he know about second chances ---

and how most of us never get past that?
what does he know about being in love

with two different people of different worlds,
and wishing it was one and the same person?
what does he know about finally wanting to move on
--- but have something hold you back?
and always looking over your shoulder,
just in case
someone might have followed...

...what you have been trying to say all
these years?

THE ONE©

The one you can be friends with forever.

The one who got away.
The one you wish you got to know better.
The one you think of at dawn or early morning,

and then again

At twilight,

just as the sun is setting.

The one you never really had,

or was never yours in the first place.

The booty call guy.

The one who has all the answers.

The one without a face, or with many,

who seems to know you best.

The one who means everything to you.

The one who thinks you're everything for him.

Which one?

THROW IT OUT *THERE©*

It was such a relief to be able to have
That little talk
With uhhh, the beach
The sunset,
the wind,
the sea...

They all heard what I had to say

It felt so silly
Being alone, like that In the water
At twilight

And telling them how
I was falling in love with
Someone I don't know
That it may well have been anyone out there
And I have no idea who

It was more agonizing, though,
To wonder
Whether that same person was
Falling in love with me too...
But then again,
we never really know, right?

Only the beach knows.

My NUMBERS©

Do you know how old I am?
Too old to know what's right and wrong.
Do you know how long my mother carried
my twin and I in her womb?
Nine months.
Do you know how long my father has been working for our
family?
Until now.
If that doesn't mean anything to you,
it means the whole world to me.
Do you know how long our family has been together?
Forever.
Do you still want my number?

P.S. Do you know how long I've stopped worrying
about winning and keeping score?
Too long.

After all, how can I walk away
feeling like I've lost,

When the score is
(For) 4-0 (Love)?

BLESSED©

I feel so blessed at this time

At this moment,
Right now.

Whoever you are,

Thank you for giving me this much

For showing me what good

there is around me

For making me feel alive
For letting me laugh, and cry, and go
crazy at times
For making me happy.
I hope that makes you happy too.

You already know what song

there is inside my heart,

That is,

Because you're singing the same song.

If you are who I think you are,
Then why didn't we have these conversations
Before?

Yet, we may have had these conversations before.
Only, I didn't know It was you.

I guess I am hoping In a way
That you are someone
I am wishing you to turn out to be...

But the other part of me

Wants you
To stay as a stranger.

Happy birthday,

Stranger.

In case I missed it.

CONVERSATIONS *(We Never Had)*©

LUNA

I asked what your favourite drink was.
You said, eau de vie.
Literally, water of life.

I always knew you had a thirst for life.

STELLA

I left home and arrived in this
strange land,
Seven years to this day.
I left my heart there, with you.
I was trying to run
away from you.
And from what might have been, Us,
What never was.

That was a lifetime ago.
Where did the time go?
Oh yes, that.
Graduation, Dining out, Beach, Clubs and Drinking, Broken
Relationships, Engagement, Marriage, Kids.

What happened?
Life happened.

Somehow, you knew everything I
went through.
You were watching the whole time.

And somehow, I forgot.
I never noticed you there.

LUNA
I was.
Always was.
But such is life.
You move on.
We grow up.
And grow old.

STELLA
Sometimes I wondered,
"Where are you?
I need to talk to you."
And I never got an answer.
If you were there, why didn't you say something?

LUNA
Silence.

STELLA
You're doing it again.

LUNA
Silence.

STELLA
Did life happen to you too?
Did it get so busy that you simply forgot,
That you just never had the time to
think about it.
About us, our friendship.

LUNA
You remember, don't you?
The farther I am, the less bright my light may be.
And so it is with you,
I knew you were there. Even if I didn't see you.

STELLA
Waiting in the darkness,
I wondered if you did
see me or hear me.

LUNA
Do you see these? The craters on my face?
Every moment, every milestone, every
special day you had, I had it imprinted
on me.
I did, I saw you and heard you.

STELLA
I feel like we have had this conversation before.

LUNA
Yes?
We speak through distance. And across time.

DISCOVERY©

Look at me.

Cast your eyes upon me.

Look up and let my eyes speak to you.

Let me smell your lingering scent

Let me savour you

Let me listen to your

sweet voice

Let me touch you

Let me sense you in the air, in

my every breath.

For you ---

you have managed to escape me.

So I ---

I crept back in. And dimmed out all of my lights.

Hidden but not gone,

I wait...

...For you to smell me,

taste

me,

hear

me, feel

me.

Can you see me?

Find me.

Those Eyes©

Good morning, rain.

Thank you for this day. It wasn't exceptional, but it was okay. I feel better every day and feel I'm progressing, though slowly.

At the back of my mind, I see this one person who is trying to help me and support me in my struggles through each and every day. In my mind's eye, I imagine this person having great love for me. I imagine he appreciates everything I do and think and feel and am. I imagine he loves everything that I love, everyone I love. I imagine he accepts me for all that I am, with or without the masks I used to have, with all the ugliness and bitterness of my past, with the uncertainty of my future with him. I imagine that he is there all the time – waiting, protecting me, smiling, and knowing I love him back.

Through the darkness though, I cannot see his face. So I imagine this man with a thousand faces, a voice I recognise but cannot quite remember, and a warmth that only he can give me. So I glance at him again, wondering. It dawns on me then that throughout the whole journey, we've been moving slowly, carefully towards each other - never exactly knowing when or how - but with hope in our hearts that the moment is near. We've been bound to come together, and now I'm beginning to see him. And then us.

Suddenly, a bright yellow light blinds me momentarily.

Those eyes - I've seen them before. Those were tired eyes, eyes that are swollen from crying and eyes that have seen a lot of pain – eyes that I knew have seen forever and lost it. Those eyes – they were like my own. Those eyes are learning to look towards the light amidst the darkness. There was so much hope in those eyes.

So I stared at them for a brief moment.
And then I saw those eyes speak.

They said, "I have loved you for years and forever will."

How I love those eyes.

WHO DO YOU *LOVE?©*

I love God.

I love my family, immediate and extended.

I love my friends, old and new.

I love myself... Hihihi.

I love food.

I love poetry.

I love stars... the cosmos.

I love the colour green and other citrus colors.

I love lavender too.

I love the beach.

I love white --- anything white.

I love pictures.

I love my bed.

I love the moon.

I love doughnuts, even without a hole in the middle. I
love books.
I love painting --- wish I could.

ANNA LEAH LUNA-RAVEN

I love the mole on my foot.

I love sunrise and sunset.

I love the rain and the sun.

I love our hut and our hammock in the backyard.

I love butterflies.

I love shoes.

I love girly stuff.

I love kids.

I love watching films.

I love ice cream.

I love my little notes.

I love alcohol --- I miss it.

I love looking into other people's eyes.

I love Sooky-lala moments.

I love surprises.

I love smiling.

I love cartoons.

I love hugs and cuddles.

I love candles.

I love the numbers 2 5 and 8.

I love the letters A and J.

I love new pens and paper.

I love music.

I love pyjamas.

I love my phone.

I love Winnie the Pooh and Friends.

I love weekends.

Hhhmmm, I
love you.

Yes, you.

𝒥𝐹 𝒯𝐻𝐸 𝒮𝐻𝒪𝐸 FITS©

Recently, it's been a series of trial and error for me. I never quite know how, but it feels like trying on a new dress, or getting the right hairstyle, choosing the healthiest possible food, putting on the right amount of make-up, or finding the right shoe.

One Size Fits All

Hopefully, I wouldn't have to spend that much (time, money, effort), just to find that perfect pair... the one that you could wear with anything and on different occasions... the one you're most comfortable with in which your feet wouldn't hurt... the one that says, "I can take you anywhere" or "We'll go places.."

Maybe I need one with lights on the heels so he'll be able to find me.

And then, there's that shoe that you just can't afford – the one you wish you could take home. Or have forever. But, end up staring at for the rest of your life... Or be willing to pay the price for.

They say that anything that's worth having is worth fighting for. But then again, they say too, that if you love someone, let him go. If he comes back, then he's yours forever.

I now understand what Cinderella must have gone through.

Not all stories, though, are fairytales. Not all stories have a happy ending. Not everybody finds the other glass slipper. Or fits the glass slipper.

Oh well, back to the shops then.

Wow, a horseshoe.

MAYBE©

They say that in life there are no accidents.
Maybe.

Maybe, there only are little things carefully put together, pieces of who you were and who you are that can lead you to who you may become.

Maybe God places certain people in our lives and lets specific events happen to let you know certain things and then teach you some. Maybe these people are those you see every day - the driver the Uber you're riding, the kid you see around the corner begging for spare change or food, the old lady you see at the church in the front pew every single Sunday, a cousin, an old friend, your family. It could be anyone.

Maybe even the ants that slowly creep up your arm are there to teach you something.

And then there are the little insignificant events that you would have otherwise missed had you not been so observant. Maybe you fell down the stairs for a reason, maybe the lights went out to tell you something, maybe the rain fell or the wind blew just to give you a special message, or maybe the song on the radio is already a clue you chose to ignore.

Maybe all of these are connected. Maybe all of these are bits and pieces of the one great, big puzzle you are soon to solve. Maybe all of these are connected to you.

Maybe God puts you in specific situations to make you realise that you should not let life just slip you by. Maybe God wants your attention, and wants you to look more closely, listen more intently, and be sensitive enough to everything around you.

Maybe God wants you to put special value on every person in your life and every day that you are here, wherever you are.. In all this, God has a special reason.

Maybe, God just wants you to be happy.

GOT *TIME?* ©

Remember all the things you didn't do
And believed you didn't have the time
Nor had the energy for?
Now you do.
Don't waste it.

Say you miss them.
Show how much you love
and appreciate them.
Create, don't hate.
Relate, don't procrastinate.
Before fate makes you lose it again..
Life and Love in the time of Covid.

We'll never be the same again.
This is the new normal.
Connect, through whatever means,

Like taking the time

to read this poem to a friend.

Got time now?

~ to the moon and back ~

"Tell me the story again about how the sun loved the moon so much that he died every night to let her breathe"

Anonymous

MOONEY's SPECIAL MAGICAL SECRET GARDEN©

I woke up at exactly 12 noon today
I hated myself for getting up so late, hey.
Lunch was already cooked by Mama,
and it smelt so wonderful,
But I had to get away.

My secret was waiting.

I have a secret --- a garden.
One which my Papa and Mama do not know about,
One that even my siblings know nothing of.
Only I knew about my secret garden.

I never had a flair for words,
So let me tell you in the best way I could ---
A poem about a family
Called GOOD.

Joe was Papa, Martha was Mama
Will was the eldest, followed by Estelle, yes.
Then the twin girls came, Nina and Sam were their names
And Ben was last of all, but boy oh boy, was he tall.

The kids' names, as you may have noticed without a
doubt, Stood for NEWS: North, East, West and South.
For this, little Ben sometimes got teased as he stood out,
For the first letter of his name did not begin with any of these,
and so he pouts.

But B for Ben is like in-Between:
the Northeast, Northwest, Southwest, Southeast.
Always in middle of conversations and commotion, he is very keen
Bright and bubbly, though not quite sure of himself, life of the family --- he is all of these.

They lived in a farm
Called The Good Autumn Farm.
And everything about it
Was nice and neat, it was such a retreat.

Everything belonged in its place
The farm was huge, there was so much space.
The soil of the land was rich,
Of all the fruits and veggies there, I could not pick which.

The farm was scattered with different plants
A pineapple patch, pumpkins, coconut, mango and guava trees
The only annoying thing were the ants
And the busy buzzing of the bees

Life was good, and such was life,
Said Joe the husband to his dear wife
The whole family was as happy as can be
Singing Lalalalala... Oh, dear me!

They had a big farm house
With an east and west wing
All the kids' bedrooms were upstairs,
Except for young Ben's, the poor thing.

There were goats and chickens, pigs and cows,
Horses, birds, ducks, and a resident mouse.
There was Stupid, the dog and Sharp, the cat
Now, you probably know why they called them that.

They had neighbours too here and there,

And you'll see them at the annual fair.
There were the Donovans, the O'Reillys,
the McKinleys, The Smiths,
the Clarkes and the Kennedys.

There was also The Upper Hut, a pub
For old women and men, it was a hub
Serving ale, and pies, and other stuff
In and out, people came, and believe me, there was enough.

I, Nina, was the naughtiest of the lot,
Avoid getting into trouble I could not
I would escape and look around the pub,
Wondering why old people liked ale,
maybe someday I would get there a job.

Yesterday, I borrowed the wagon from Papa,
Cause I was already running late to meet a friend for a cuppa
But I got distracted thinking of flying dragons
And guess what, into a big rock, the wagon smashed head on.

This was when Papa and Mama told me I was grounded
inside the house,
And I didn't like it for a minute,
oh noes, I said, especially not now.
That meant I couldn't see my lovely secret garden,
So I decided to write, my favourite thing to do,
and took my paper and pen.

Then, I sneaked out the back door
Oh, was it magical and so much more!
I went south of the riverbank,
and then west where the sun sets
Alas, I was out of the house!
So, go to the secret garden, let's!

As I was Good with directions (get it?),
I worked my way in a land with forest, hills and streams,
I was running and walking and
having fun going through the motions,

About this beautiful garden,
stringing some wonderful dreams.

I drew my own map of how to get to this special place,
It was easy to read, I understood the tracks and pathways
I was in no chase, and on the way I played
I will name it Mooney, said I, as I went on my own pace

And there it was...
The Secret. The Garden.
My Special Magical Secret Garden.

At the entrance was a cloud of petunias on my feet
Scattered like soft dotted colors of pinks and
violets and yellows
Oh, the scents! Make my heart skip a beat
It's here, all true, I can say now my mind is not hollow.

There were Old English roses, the Bourbons and the Gallicas,
The David Austin roses in full bloom
Wild lavender and underneath it, Watercress grass
You can barely tell of the past that was then gloom.

Towards the left side of the garden was an arbor,
Fully covered in Wisteria blossoms
Intermingled with the occasional clematis, how I adore!
Oh everything, all of it, just filled from way up to
down the bottom.

Dandelions flying like pinwheels everywhere,
Taking all of my worries and cares,
And as I go in further into the secret garden,
Lovely flowers abound, no longer hidden.

Larkspurs, Delphiniums, and Stargazer Lilliums,
Bluebells, Tulips and Daffodils scattered all around Every
Orchid that you can think of and Malaysian Mums,
Daisies and Carnations --- new varieties I've found.

There was on the right, a wishing well,
Whether it was filled with water I could not tell,
Birds flew and squirrels ran around the field,
I could not be happier, my spirit is healed.

Oh what a wonderful sight this heavenly delight,
I stayed there so long I didn't notice it was almost night
Sunset is on the horizon,
And I better head back home soon.

Then something suddenly struck me,
I realized I had my own secret garden to go back to
My family is a special secret garden --- I love my family
Of different plants we make up the whole garden through

Papa was strong and sturdy as a tree,
Mama was like a flower making everything
beautiful and smell good too
The garden makes us feel good and alive and (sometimes) free,
They make up the most important parts, these two.

We, the children, were like the fruits
Stemming from trees and flowers,
Waiting to grow, waiting to be ready to be picked from our
roots
We were apples and oranges, bananas, peaches, and pears.

Then I looked up, saw a glimpse of the shining moon and the
first star in the sky,
Wondering and pondering what they would be saying
to each other
If they had the words in my mind's eye,
With these thoughts, I go home and say "maybe bother later…"

In the meantime, will you keep this secret,
About our special magical garden?
Nobody knows it yet
Except you, my secret friend.

THE 𝒰𝒩𝒥𝒞𝒪𝒭𝒩 SPELL©

Eight (8) Ingredients for a Unicorn

a horse's golden hair
a dove's white feather

sweets: fairy fluff, bubblegum and sugar candy sprinkles

soap bubbles
jewels

rainbow tears (raindrop)

dried scented colorful flowers
...and, salt for good measure

A unicorn, I wish to make

So these gifts I have, please do take

A good friend to it I wish to be
And it be so a friend to me

A horse's golden hair is here

To clothe its glorious body dear

I bring a dove's white feather
To make it fly, above and yonder

These sweets I offer

Fairy fluff, Bubble gum and sugar candy sprinkles

So this bright and bubbly creature
Will always tug at my heart and make me tingle

It will float lightly like a soap bubble
And will always get me out of trouble
A wonderful colorful hit
when the light shines through it

Jewels to crown her horn, I bring
And to match her eyes a-sparkling
Golden, shining, majestic and bright
It will be such a beautiful sight

It will be a sign of good times
Like when the rainbow shines,
But to make it feel human, a raindrop
So it knows when to pop up and when to stop

Flowers will make it a sight to behold
But no one must be told,
Of this scented beauty
Which I promise to keep secretly

Have a lifetime friend, only a lucky few do
Make my wish come true
I call it magic, do you hear?
A unicorn do appear!

GRATITUDE©

Thank you.

For GOD
For prayer
For life
For family
For home
For friends
For childhood
For school
For learning
For work
For earning
For time
For being alone

For being around people

For help
For peace of mind
For fullness of heart
For a calm soul
For a free spirit
For leisure
For words
For laughter
For song
For voice
For myself
For sight, smell, sound, taste, touch
For body
For heat, For cold

For water

For air

For sunshine
For moonlight
For stars
For love

For you.
For heartaches
For tears
For memories

For past
For future
For now.

banana©

smile for me.

wipe out that frown. ☹

Flip, flop.

Thud, my heart did drop.

Flop, flip.

Boom, my heart skipped a beat.

wipe out that frown.

smile for me. (❀´‿`❀)

FOUR SEASONS©

My most favorite day

Is the day

I met you.

Secret©

Can I tell you

a secret?

You are mine.

ᗰᗩY ᗰOOᑎ HAIKU©

So what do you say
Let's celebrate but first pray
My whole soul I lay

Beautiful Fall day
Back garden, rolling in hay
Hear the horses neigh

Look, Setting sun's rays
Hear songs of the mockingjay
Saying goodnight, hey

Five haikus I say
A lovely homage to pay
With me, come and stay

Special day in May
The moon and stars seem to play
For it's my birthday

NIGHT DANCE©

Let us dance under
the light of the moon and the
twinkling of the stars
In the vast Night Sky.

Let us forget all our
worries,
away from all of
our cares.

Let us make believe we
are alone

In the world
Let us just be here, not there.

CONNECT

Thank you

I love you

I'm sorry

I'm not perfect

I will ask for help when I need it

I can see now

Hello I want to be your friend

I miss you

Happy Birthday, in case I missed it

How are you today?

LUNA AND STELLA©

I guess I have been sitting here for a while now, but I don't mind at all. I have been doing this for as long as I can remember.

"Oh, where would she turn up this time?" and "I wonder how she would look like?" I always ask myself in my wait.

Just hours ago I had to sneak away from Papa and Mama just so I could get a glimpse of her. Every night before going to sleep I have been doing just that and it still excites me. But tonight --- tonight was special. I had some questions I needed to ask her.

Khalil, the wind, was blowing gently tonight, and it had become unusually quiet, as if everything in the world was preparing for what was about to happen; everything suspended in anticipation. And then, it happened.

Sol had just waved goodbye to everyone and disappeared into the twilight, almost taking with her the light from all around. Suddenly, just from out of the corner of my eye, I saw her. As always she was a beauty. Oh how I adore her!

Ever so softly, Luna, with her glowing smile, crept up the sky, bringing in a soft, almost dreamy translucence to everything again. Tonight, she chose the northeast.

"Luna!" I gasped in awe.

And then she smiled at me. She knew I was waiting for her.

Her face was full with big, bright eyes that had a silver sparkle. Beneath it, she had creamy skin that was sprinkled with silver dust. All of her features were illuminated, like it was always whenever she had this face on. Her lips were shapely, almost pouting, and her cheeks were a blush of pale blue. Her nose sort of looked stubby in this face though. But she was still very beautiful. Everything about her seem to shine through.

"Ahhh, there you are," she said when she saw me. "I was beginning to wonder where you might be."

"Oh Luna, you know I am always waiting for you to come out." Hmmm, is that right?"

"Why, are you getting tired of me waiting up for you and chatting?"

"Of course not sweetie. In fact, I always look forward to our nocturnal tete-a-tete." "Really?"

"Really."

And then I paused. I didn't know how I would bring up the questions I had wanted to ask her. Now that she has arrived, I'm feeling a bit ashamed.

"What's wrong? I know you, and you know you can always talk to me. So, tell me..." "Well, it's just that I, uhhh..."

'Uhummm..." she prodded me on.

"Well, I have been waiting a long time to ask you something. But now I don't know if it's alright."

"I'm sure whatever it is, I can find an answer to. And if I cannot, we'll have to go figure out together, won't we?"

"I guess..." and then a pause again.

"I was just wondering, you know --- can anyone see me?"

"Does anyone see me at all?"

Silence.

So I went on. "I'm getting older, see, and I don't feel like others know me as they do Orion, or am as colourful as Galatea, or shoot like Hyperion. I'm not as big the twins Triton and Titan, nor do I twinkle like Ganymede. I don't think there's something special about me, Luna."

I didn't quite know what I saw on Luna's face at that moment, but it seemed to me that she was... sad. There was a look of whimsy in her eyes that I could not see through or understand. It was as if she was thinking, carefully composing, scripting what she was going to tell me.

I had always looked up to Luna because she was so beautiful, not only by reason that she had the brightest light of us all among the heavenly bodies of the night sky, but also for she had a certain wisdom that only the years of staying here in Solaris could bring. Stars such as myself are born year in and out, but Luna --- she has been here forever. I have been coming to her for stories before bedtime when I was much smaller and much younger, and up to now, though some stories may have changed, I still come to her. Other times though, it was I who told her stories, or I would listen to her sing soothing lullabies...

"I see the moon
and the moon sees me,
and the moon sees somebody I want to see.

God bless the moon
and God bless me,
and God bless the somebody I want to see.

God looked down from up above,
and He picked you out for me to love.
He picked you out from all the rest,
cause He knew that I'd love you the very best."

Or, we'd simply sit together without exchanging words. Sometimes I come to her for advice, and she has never failed and coming up with the best answers to my every question or enquiry, no matter what situation. She was my mentor, my best friend.

But tonight, I had a feeling she was dumbstruck, too overwhelmed. Tonight, for the first time, I think she had no answer.

"Oh, Stella..." was all she could mutter in a whisper.

We sat there in silence again. This time it felt really awkward. I think she sensed it too.

Finally, she said, "You feel invisible, is that it?"

That was it. That was exactly how I felt. That was exactly the word for it. So I nodded in agreement.

"You feel completely alone, even when you're not? You feel lost, don't you?"

"I guess I do," I answered.

"Sometimes, you can be with or around others who can make you feel that way."

Silence. I was waiting for her to go on.

"But you know what? Maybe that's the exact same reason why you and me, we are here together in the vast night sky... to remind us that we need others around us who truly see and understand us. We might not see each other that often. Oftentimes, I may be hiding behind clouds, and you, like the other stars, may be too far away from me. But then again, we find comfort in knowing that somewhere out there, there are others who are going through the same things that we do... that somewhere out there, someone is feeling lonely, or growing weak, or can't seem to find their inner light."

I was listening intently.

"Somewhere out there, someone might be feeling just a wee bit too big, others a wee bit too small. One feeling awkward about being too big for her own size, her flaws get noticed all the time... while the other, feeling unappreciated and craving for attention, feeling too small to be acknowledged. One being too near, and the other too far. One desperately trying to be just like the other, the other looking out for someone who might think they're special enough to make a wish on."

"Is that true, Luna?" I was trying to grasp what she just revealed.

"Yes. Do you understand?" she inquired, knowing fully well I now did. I hated the fact that she always throws questions back at me.

"Is that you, Luna?" I finally asked.

"Now, do you see me too, Stella?" Yes, another question. She was having a go at me, having fun with this inquisition.

I looked at her, smiled, and replied, "I see you." I see all of you, Luna. I see how patient you are with my million questions. I see your wisdom in the answers and advice you give me. I see how beautiful you see the world, and that's what makes you beautiful too. I see how you make the night feel still and peaceful and calm with your guiding light. Yet, I see how tired you are, being up all night, watching over the whole night sky. I see how you love what you do though, as your light is exactly the same intensity when you come out and when you go, because you

never really go. You are always there. I see you're my only

friend. And sometimes, that is enough."

"Thank you." I thought I saw a tear in her eye. "I see all of you too, Stella. I see me in you."

Silence. We just looked at each other for a moment.

"I guess it's not only you who has all the answers." I teased.

And then we both laughed.

The truth is, we did figure it out together, me and Luna. I started humming again...

"I see the moon
and the moon sees me,
and the moon sees somebody I want to see.

God bless the moon and
God bless me, and
God bless the somebody I want to see.

God looked down from up above,
and He picked you out for me to love.
He picked you out from all the rest,
cause He knew that I'd love you the very best."

~ shoot for the moon ~

"Shoot for the moon. Even if you miss, you'll land among the stars."

Les Brown

MANTRAS©

Do not sleep as much as you can. Get just enough sleep. There are too many things waiting to be done or discovered out there to be wasted on sleeping.

Get a good digital camera or video cam. Every moment deserves to be remembered, and sometimes our memory isn't as reliable. Take photographs --- lots of them. Make or create a scrapbook too while you're at it.

Have a mobile phone so that no matter where you are or what you're doing you stay connected.

Write. Whatever it is that's on your mind, put it on paper. You never know when your memory will fail you. Plus, it's good therapy

Try everything at least once... anything at all!

Pick out a favourite song <u>and</u> a favourite poem, and know them by heart.

Try to be friends with your ex's. You'll know why when both of you start laughing at the memories. Less awkward moments.

Smile. It's good facial exercise, lessens wrinkles.

Watch at least one sunset and at least one sunrise. You'll be surprised how much you crave for more. This time, though, ignore your mobile phone... unless you're capturing the beauty you see.

Have a good, warm jacket handy. You'll never know when it rains.

If you can't say anything good, it's best not to say anything at all. Never criticize, be polite.

Always be good, even if others are not. See the good in every person, or at least try, and believe it. No man is naturally evil. Do not lose faith in people.

Pray. Once when you wake up, once before and after meals, once before going to sleep, and then in between... on your way to work, while washing the dishes, as you exercise or watch a movie, while taking a shower, while reading a book... every minute you can.

Listen to the rain. Stay in bed during a storm.

Have a makeshift camp-out site inside your room, just in case you don't feel like sleeping on your bed.

Clean as you go.

Marry someone you really, truly love. If you can't, marry someone who loves you more.

Aside from the jacket, always keep a book handy. You never know when you'll have to pass time.

Read, read, read. You just might learn something new.

Remember important dates or events – birthdays, anniversaries, graduations, baby's first word.

Remember your firsts. First crush, first kiss, first love... And pray that you'll get to keep your last.

Make friends with a stranger.

Eat lots of fruits and vegetables. Your mum was right.

Sing a song when you feel good. Sing a song when you feel bad.
Just sing, even if you don't know the words. Humming is good
too.

Start a collection like I do. Stars!

If someone breaks your heart, open it up again. Who knows,
the one you let inside might turn out to be a repairman.

Do not leave things hanging.

Try to quit smoking. At least try.

Buy a hammock.

Talk to your parents. Hug them. Kiss them.

Do not stalk your crushes. Hahaha.

Forgive anyone who has done you wrong.

Try to not drool while sleeping.
Make fun of yourself once in a while.

Pamper yourself. Even just lighting a candle can be soothing.

Have a journal.

Clean your room.

Get a pet, whether cold-blooded or warm-blooded. As long as it
reminds you how to be responsible for someone or something.
Send out good vibes. Everyday.

WINGS©

Why do we look up
when we look at the moon?

I want to be with you,
Up there, with you.

Like stars, who share in your
company, in June

Give me wings,
To take on flight
Pearls on string
Bring me up to the light
So I can have my dream

Of being with you

KEEPING IT *REAL©*

So, is integrity something
measureable?

When it comes down to who said
What, When and Where,
do the How and Why have a chance?

When it comes down to their word against
mine,
Does it really matter how
many times Someone lied?

Or does intent make all the difference?

#WAR OF *WORDS*©

Gaslighting.
Bagging.
Gossiping.
They put you down.
Is this fair to you?
Is it?

Acknowledgment.
Encouragement.
Reward.
They lift you up.
Isn't this what's fair to you?
Isn't it?

Strike now.
Strike with a pen.
Not with a sword.
Not with violence,
not with aggressiveness,
not with assault.
Not with demonstrations,
not with attacks,
not with hits.

War on words. War of Words.
This is what needs to be done.
Take to the streets (or sheets)
And have your thoughts known.

The pen is so powerful.
You can make money from it.
You can make time stop or slow
down with it.

You can get more power from it.

Revolution.

Seek truth.
And not rumours.
Spread truth.
And don't gossip.
Shine the light on truth.
And be truth itself.

Seek justice.
Not Inequity.
Spread love. Not hate, nor apathy.
Spread fairness. Not prejudice.
Seek openness.

Get out of that damn box.

Think outside the box.
Scribble.
    Draw.
     Write.

Social Media.
Youtube.
The Web.
Internet.
Vlogs.
#Hashtags.

Embrace
change.
Embrace the
future.
Embrace
you, me, us.

Change our
future.

This is the wave of the future...
The pen, the mouse.
The digital camera, the android phone.
The laptop, the tablet.

Create.
Live.
Enjoy.
Play...

A War of Words. Or images.

Think.
And make people do the same.
Challenge...

The status quo.
Share knowledge,
Because knowledge is
power.
Share...

Your time, money, effort.
These are essential
investments
For a fair future.
Build...

Relationships, And communities.
And a positive culture.
Teach, and learn, and interact.
Through words...

A War of Words,

No... a play on words.

Let us build a unified, free, fair world
without boundaries or divisions
By empowering change through words or images
we use everyday.

Aren't you tired?
Instead of fighting and struggling,
why not play?
Be free...
to write and draw,
scribble and snap.
Come and play. And maybe stay.
Stay awhile, let us talk.
Let us speak our truths.
Let us listen to other truths.
Let us exchange, let us be fair.

Practice fairness and equality.
Use your mighty pen.
Imagination included.
Post it out there.
Let it flow out of you.
Practice makes perfect.
Voice out your thoughts and opinions.
And be heard.
Don't be scared,
I am with you.

"Mirror, mirror on the wall,
Who's the fairest of them all?"
First, Australia.
Then the whole world.

I WISH©

I hope and pray that I'll always feel good,
That my family's always safe and healthy and happy.

I wish there were less mean people in the world,
Who would like to make other people's
lives difficult and miserable.

I wish there was enough love to
go around the world

And peace, and happiness.

I wish I can be good all the time.

I wish I can make people happy.

I wish I didn't feel so bad all the time.
I wish I had a big eraser that could erase all my mistakes,
And make them all turn into good things.
That would make everything better.
I wish I wouldn't be such a drama queen all the time.
I wish I didn't lie before
Because it feels so good just telling the truth.

I wish I could live forever

So I can live out my days

Making up for all the bad things I've done.

I wish I didn't scare people away.
Because that scares me.
I wish I wasn't so scared all the time.

I wish I could be more realistic.
People live on earth, not the moon.

$\mathcal{BE}_{©}$

Be a friend,

and then sweep her off her feet.

Be a star,

so she will always have someone to look up to,

Whenever she loses her way.

And then guide her back home to you.

QUESTIONS©

Sometimes,
getting the right answers
Does not matter as much
As asking the right questions.

SMILE©

I hope I can put

A permanent smile

On your face,

Even if it means having to lose mine.

BACK TO YOU

I will always go back
to you.

Whenever I get lost,
I will always find my way back to you.

I'm sorry I didn't get to visit
you today.

Please know you will always
have my heart.

I'm sorry I failed
you today.

Please greet me with a cool breeze
and warm sunshine tomorrow,

Like you always do.

Thank you for a clear
night tonight.
I can see my stars.

I lost my book.

That's the closest thing I have

To talking to you anytime I want.

I hope I find it.

Is it back with you?

KEEP DREAMING©

Keep dreaming,
my child.

Keep your
dreams alive.

What do you want to be when you grow up?

I want to have
a house
Of my own.

I want
a love
Of my own.

I want
a family
Of my own.

Stop dreaming, child.

Now's the day

To make dreams come true.

No hurry, child.

We will eventually get there...

To forever.

A LETTER TO MY
FUTURE CHILDREN©

Dear Children,

> My most special daughters,

> And my most special sons,

You know who you are. I will not mention or write down your names anymore, because apart from the fact that I know them by heart, I feel like those names are, like you, so fragile and should be handled with the utmost care and like newborn babies, only respond to the softest, gentlest, most loving touch.

...And while I am looking forward to hearing myself calling you by them, and other people using them to address or refer to you, I would rather save it for the best and most appropriate and most opportune – the perfect – time...

Let this letter also be a way of saying I am truly sorry... because,

> I see your beautiful faces looking at and looking back at me with so much anticipation and longing.

> I see your wonderful smiles that give me hope to face a brand new day, and give me reassuring comfort at the end of a long one.

> I see your bright eyes sparkle and glow at the thought of us being all together.

I see your tiny, little arms reaching out for a touch, a warm hug (though it be in my mind).

I feel your warm love envelope me as much as it overwhelms you.

...And know that, though these dreams have become, and still are real to me, I succumb to the fact that I do not have control over certain things and circumstances.

...And am not quite sure if, and when, I would be able to breathe you into life, into reality. Or someone else will.

And although it is true that we each make our own fate, I also believe that it is but right to let nature take its own course --- that it is only through the same, destiny, that we realize which particular road to take.

So with this, I pray that ---
However long time takes,
However far away the horizon is,
However difficult or painstaking
The journey will be,
However futile
or senseless the reasons
May seem to be,
Whatever obstacles
I go through,

--- Under no circumstances will I stop trying.

...If only to utter your names,
If only to put a face behind
those names,
If only to put a smile on
those faces,

If only to look into
those eyes,
If only to feel
your love,
Through those arms
that I try to reach out to as well...

...This time, for real.

~~~

Speak to me,
I want to
know what you
are thinking,
feeling,
I want to bare
my soul, as you
do yours.
I don't
know how
to survive
without
this
I want to know all
of it, what was,
what is,
and what might have been.
Let me know you, and
me. And the whole world
that's between us.

ABOUT THE *Author*

Anna Leah Luna-Raven is an emerging writer from Perth, Western Australia. She grew up and spent most of her adult years in the Philippines, until she immigrated to Australia to be with her then fiance, and now husband, back in 2012. She grew up in a Catholic family, and she graduated from the University of the Philippines with a Communications degree. She began writing at a very young age.

Anna's latest works include: "...oh, I don't know..." published on an online literary journal, Lite Lit One, and "cab thoughts: EMP-ty" published on an LGBTIQA+ magazine, Bent Street 3.

Her work, "The Surprise Party" (also known as "Random Rantings - PLEASE add me as a friend if you're NOT..."), was also chosen as one of the works to be performed in the Voices of Women podcast. Another poem, "Got Time?" was shown on the Big Screen at Northbridge Piazza for the 2020 Perth Poetry Festival. Her poem, "Like The Moon Loves The Stars in The Sky", was also published on Snowdrops, a Wingless Dreamer publication.

Connect with Me

facebook

instagram

Linktree✳

linktr.ee

Made in the USA
Columbia, SC
10 May 2024

35017268R00078